Braised in wine

D.D. Holland

V.

Published in the United Kingdom in 2023
by V. Press,
10 Vernon Grove,
Droitwich,
Worcestershire,
WR9 9LQ.

ISBN: 978-1-7398838-5-0

Cover & inside drawings: © D.D. Holland, 2023
Cover design & inside layout: © Sarah Leavesley, 2023
Printed in the U. K. on FSC accredited paper by 4edge Limited, www.4edge.co.uk/

Acknowledgements & Trigger Warnings

*Some of these poems cover issues like eating disorders, suicidal thoughts and abuse that
some readers may find disturbing. A full list can be found at the back of this pamphlet.*

*With massive thanks to the University of Worcester, Ruth Stacey for one powerful lecture,
Jack McGowan for his remarkable patience, and Sarah Leavesley for this fantastic
opportunity. With special thanks to David Swann. My mother (who actually makes very
nice food), my father (for listening), the rest of my family (who provide good material),
and my Vo, without whom I would starve (poetically and literally).*

Contents

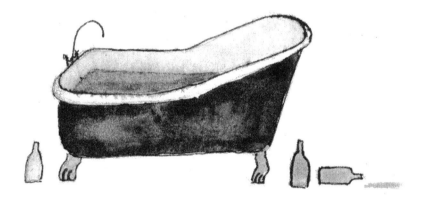

An Excuse to Eat Bolognese

When life throws you off the horse, you have four options.
Walk away, get back on, make bolognese,
that or put the fucking thing up for adoption.
When I fall off a horse, I like to choose option three.
That way you're a horse down, but a bolognese up.
And all the other horses know how scared they should be.

A Knife and Fork

It is under the buzz of fluorescent lights
that she dissects her monster.
The offending organ is amputated,
(the patient lies
silently haemorrhaging).
It is placed on a stainless steel tray
to cough and gutter
before it falls still.
The silver platter is pushed across the table to you,
where you wait,
with a knife and fork,
to complain that your meal is too bitter.

Bitter Lemons

Bitter lemons are sweet to me.
Onions make me smile and
chilli is the gentlest kiss.

My world spins on the axis
of his finger, and is pounded
to crumbs by his fist.

My Big Sister

I used to like eggs
but she didn't like eggs,
so our father used to make us chicken burgers
before he drove her home.

She drank Ribena,
while I scattered rusk crumbs and wetted the carpet.
My curls straightened into 90s shards;
she watched *Gladiator* and texted her boyfriend.
I drank her Ribena.

She likes Earl Grey tea
and the room feels awkward because
I've never said I love her
and we sip in veritable silence.

She likes Earl Grey tea.
I like Earl Grey tea.
I still don't like eggs.

The Last Supper

My mother keeps me alive by making shit food.
Tonight, it's casserole.
Vegetables boiled in water until all taste evaporates
but the potatoes are still hard.
I spoon it into my mouth with poorly concealed misery and think:
this is no Last Supper.
I'll have to try again tomorrow,
only tomorrow it's stir-fry from the shop,
which always tastes like plastic packets.
I'll have to try again tomorrow.

When I eat a pizza with soft crusts and cheese stringing off the edges
like dairy icicles,
alongside all the weird toppings I add
to procure sole ownership of my pizza,
because no one else wants a slice with asparagus, goat's cheese,
olives and artichoke hearts
(plus a side of potato wedges),
I become a Buddhist monk who has found enlightenment.
Life could not possibly get any better than hot cheese pizza,
especially when it's followed by Mr. Whippy ice cream
with all the toppings.
The other noises in my head
melt away in the greasy puddles at the corner of my pizza box,
and I think:
now, would be a good time to die.
To swallow fistfuls of pills,
their bitter taste hidden in the ice cream
until I can't differentiate between a tablet
taking me 5mg closer to the abyss,
and a Skittle.
I would die, here, in the car

with tomato-stained lips
and the remnants of ice cream
souring on my tongue.

Tonight, it was curry that tasted like soap.
I'll have to try again tomorrow.

Mushrooms

He doesn't like mushrooms.
He hates the way they crawl over his tongue,
leaving slimy, buttery trails.

He's alone again, in his room – he's been there for days
and all he can think to say when dragged to the dinner table,
sick and gaunt in the face,
is that he doesn't like mushrooms.

His room is dark and damp and the air never stirs
except for the air above his finger which clicks on
grainy pictures of dark bedrooms.
What fungus grows on the untended mind?

A Bad Egg

Humpty Dumpty sat on a ward with
Humpty Dumpty's name on a board.

All the mental health nurses
and middle-aged men

couldn't put Humpty together again.

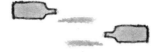

Séance

I grieve for endless bread and butter.
The kind I try to recreate when the house is empty,
but my bread is white, or worse, homemade.
Sometimes I ask for the same seeded, packaged loaf
that you used to serve in fingers
on side plates.
I butter it with Clover
(but I think you used Flora?).
It doesn't taste the same.

It doesn't taste the same
because you kept it in the fridge.
But not my fridge,
your fridge.
To make my bread taste like your bread,
I would have to recreate your fridge.
Homemade cottage cheese made from spoilt milk
and stilton to be eaten in crumbs.
Coleslaw, opened tins of baked beans,
and Kit-Kats.
No, sorry, Club bars.

But even after I have rebuilt your fridge,
it still doesn't taste the same,
because you didn't buy your bread to taste of your bread;
you brought it for your cardiovascular health,
and for the birds.

Now my fridge is full of coleslaw and blue cheese
which I can't stand,
and loaves of shop-bought seeded bread
and milk I bought purposefully so it might curdle into cheese.

My meals are the things which still taste the same.
Gingernuts dipped in ice-cold milk,
and cups of tea
which only taste authentic because I kept the right mugs,
and pizza which is frozen on the top but burnt on the bottom.

But the room smells wrong and I can't feel the fire on my knees.
Your chair doesn't sit in the corner
and no matter how hard I will it,
there are not endless supplies of anything.

I cannot make my bread taste like your bread;
your bread is gone.

The Raising Agent

She never sifts the icing sugar,
or waits for the oven to preheat.

She considers the ingredients list advisory,
uses scales to rest her wine on
and leaves food on the stovetop overnight.

Her recipe uses double the sugar,
half the butter,
and whatever she can find at the bottom of the fridge.

We used to watch each other bake,
simmering like stove pots,
until we each admitted:
she makes good cake.

Chocolate and Strawberry

She always chose chocolate; I always chose strawberry.
After a long day of fighting,
we would start work at either end of a tub of Neapolitan
and meet in the peace of banal vanilla.

But she always preferred pink, and I preferred black.
As she grew, her hair turned strawberry blonde,
and I remained brunette.

We left home.

She drove her red car south
but our black car collects speeding tickets
with northern postcodes.

She sends me videos, shivering in her pink gym kit;
I watch them at café tables in my black leather jacket,
sipping hot chocolate.

A Dog's Dinner with Dad

I haven't eaten a green bean in six years.
Because who would want to eat anything with a texture somewhere
between a wire and a wig?
The feeling of strings around my tongue makes me choke
and I want to spit out the entire mouthful,
which is a waste of potato.
I vowed to boycott green beans.
I would leave them soaking in puddles of gravy,
or hidden under the fish skin or chicken bones
like a child playing peek-a-boo.
If I can't see them, you can't see them.
Still, you continued, daily, to pile green beans alongside my carrots
and scrape them, daily, into a bowl for the dog.
Years of accumulated green-bean waste
stand behind me.
An estimated ten kilograms of squandered strings
(enough to make a wig),
until it stopped.
Now you spoon green beans on every plate but mine,
and I get my dinner first.
You hand it across the table,
and I pretend that I don't notice their absence,
or the additional scoop of mashed potato.
And you pretend you have just forgotten.
I, of course, am thrilled.
The dog, of course, is not.

Domestic Goddess

Nigella is a Domestic Goddess.
She wrote a book about it.
She cooks in black silk pyjamas,
nipples erect over the bubbling pans;
rumour has it she uses them to knead the dough.

I am not Nigella Lawson.
I cook in yesterday's socks;
I don't even own black silk pyjamas
because they're impractical.

I will marry you,
if you like.
I will be your wife and you can be my partner
but don't bother buying me black silk pyjamas
or asking me to make breakfast,
or expect to find me kneading with my breasts.

If you want eggs in the morning,
I'll buy you an apron.

Can we get takeout?

We used to be addicted to takeout.
When we first met,
we were too busy in love
to waste moments over the stove.
Tenderly unwrapped,
we ate on kitchen floors and
on the M5 while you drove
us to Leeds.

You showed me your favourite places,
and I showed you mine.
We found new ones together
but soon,
we ran out of money and time.

We settled down to the daily grind
and for the sake of our health,
we ate salad.
Maybe we got takeout once a month?
Ordering from familiar places;
although the taste was still as sweet as the first time,
it wasn't the first time anymore.

We got used to the menu,
always ordered the same thing.
We didn't share our meals
or lick the sauce off each other's skin.
Sometimes we ate together;
sometimes I finished alone.

Although, of course,
the food was good,

and we made good food at home,
I realised that at the age of twenty-one,
I had committed myself to a life
of our kind of takeout.

I know we can't go back to the way it was before,
otherwise,
we would both be pleasured,
but fat and poor.

Could we get takeout tonight?
At that new place down the street?
Could we get takeout every night this week?

The Chef of the Family

Your brother cooks like a bear hug.
When you swing your legs over the kitchen counter,
disintegrating tissues across your thighs like snowfall,
he stirs pasta in the letters of your name
and tuts in all the right places.

When your heart is breaking,
he fills the cracks with soup,
slows the poison spread by pouring
double cream into your arteries.
He takes the edge off salty tears with a spoonful of honey,
bastes you in butter, pan-fries until golden,
arranges you in neat layers and garnishes with icing sugar.
He couldn't warm you with stocky arms,
not the way he could with fresh baked bread.

I am held together by peanut butter and jam
and bear-hug bowlfuls.
I would tell him,
if I knew how to speak cheese sauce:
I love you,
I love you too.

Pregnancy Scare

I had loved you for four months.
Sat at opposite ends of the bathroom
in hysterical silence,
bloodless knickers bundled up
with yesterday's t-shirts.
"We can't keep it,"
you said.

I wrapped my arms around my belly
as though you were going to perform the extraction yourself.
Through the steam,
you could see that
you were outnumbered.

You slammed the front door
and I sat naked on the shower floor
for hurt and fear, but never again for loneliness.
I stopped crying into the drain,
comforted by the beats of a tiny, imaginary heart.
I love you, I love you, I love you.

You came back with a paper bag
that didn't contain a pregnancy test
and spoke into my empty womb
which felt so full.

In the paper bag was our usual order.
Warm fries and soft burgers
to celebrate the accidental creation of our family.
We whispered that we would hide by the docks,
holed up in the Royal Armouries, where we could
raise our monarch in secret.

In between defending our home and schooling our sovereign,
we could grow fat on breastmilk and brown paper bags.

We fused like the moment of creation,
and though you breathed when my womb turned itself inside out,
sometimes I still whisper to our
Royal Armouries Romulus.

Aphrodisiac

I used to think that skinny equalled sexy.
The skinnier you were, the sexier you were.
I tried to starve myself so sexy that I could fit into a condom.
Fatness was a dirty word,
an undesirable trait held by undesirable people.

He asked me out, the skinniest fat girl in the room,
but he had a secret
that I didn't discover until our first date,
when he became entangled in a cheese enchilada;
he eats everything like Nigella Lawson,
like it's some kind of sex show.

He moans, and closes his eyes and lets custard dribble down his lip,
plumped up deliciously by all the custard that has come before it.
I won't eat anything with sugar,
but the way the granules stick to his tongue like an arctic winter
makes my mouth water.
Fats are for people who suffer from fatness,
but his shiny, butter-soaked fingers
beg to be licked clean.
He shudders when thick cream, half-way between pourable
and spoon-able,
gets caught on his chin;
and he can do unspeakable things with a jug of gravy.
He makes it impossible to deny seconds and thirds,
only satiated when his stomach gargles in happy approval
and the spoon has been sucked clean.
Is it any surprise that I grew hungry for him?

Undressed, he rejects skinniness.
He is rounded edges, like an over-filled muffin case
and smooth as molten chocolate.
His belly is sticky toffee pudding, wallowing in extra sauce

and his skin is sweet.
His shower gel smells of candy canes, but the nape of his neck smells
like a proving drawer,
mixed with the smell of the kitchen when tender rosemary-lamb
has been roasting in the oven.
He ripples through my taste buds;
the tip of my tongue is not enough to appreciate every flavour.

At night, I reach out to him, starving.
I knead his hips
and run my tongue down his spine.
He turns, letting out a jam-roly-poly kind of moan,
and strokes my belly
which is no longer full of skinniness
but seconds.
I reach for his boxers.

What they will never know

How starving I was before I met you.
That my portion sizes doubled after our first date,
when I crammed my cheeks with apple cakes
and I couldn't decide if the alien fullness came from my bloated
stomach or my giddy head.

I went into the hospital and told them to speed up my eating plan,
because I knew you would hold my hand at Christmas dinner.
Foods I hadn't eaten since childhood stood, lined up on the table,
tin soldiers for me to defeat.
That you cooked me beans which ended up
congealed and watered down with tears.

How many times you asked me if I had eaten and I lied,
but somehow you always knew and stood at the fridge,
offering ever more complicated dishes,
until we settled on the same thing we always settled on:
as much
little
as possible.

They never saw the days you spoon-fed me on the bathroom floor,
pasta pieces scattered in the shower tray,
iodine absorbed by the bathmat.
That antibiotics lay strewn on the counter,
and you checked my tongue like
this was a 70s movie about a psychiatric ward
because I couldn't be trusted to swallow two calories on my own.
That you rubbed my aching belly until you had sanded it down
so I could almost see it as flat as you said it was.
At night, when dinner sat like a monster in my stomach,
I was desperate to evict it

but you locked me in your arms and sang softly in my ear.
You told me we were in a vacuum
and everything was weightless,
and we weren't falling like potato through an intestine,
we were flying together.

How many times you caught me before I hit the flagstones;
that I drink so much tea because its calorie-less warmth
fills my stomach like the ghost of a meal.
Or that we have to live together so I don't relapse into a matchstick
person,
and you can hear I'm still breathing.

How many nights I have begged you to leave me
and find a nice girl
who doesn't keep you up at night, crying about breakfast-time.
How many nights you dried my eyes
and lined my stomach with kisses,
and asked me to marry you,
proposing over and over again in the dark,
in your boxers,
until I laughed, spraying us both with tears,
and agreed to be your wife,
in sickness and in health.

Stuttercunt

"Cunt, cunt, cunt-
country,"
you said.
On stage,
in a tent full of children.
Gin mummies choked
on their cucumber slices.

You didn't notice.

You were playing your guitar,
where no one minds repeated notes
or staccato rhythms.

They don't understand
your mouth has to make music;
if it isn't singing,
it beatboxes.

When you tell me you love me,
one 'L' isn't enough.
I hoard each additional consonant
and pin it to myself like a stamp collection.
I wish I could show you
that I love you with six 'L's too.

Midnight Feast

I can only tell you at night,
when the air is thick with silence and sleep
and the gods of fate have left to stalk casinos and bars;
I am satisfied that they will not take you from me.
As though warm milk is a truth serum
that makes me vomit love,
I hold you and stroke your hair
lulled by soft snores
and I tell you
that I love the way you put your socks on before your pants.
That my heart dances to your rhythmic stutter
and when the words tangle on your page,
my favourite thing to do is help you unpick them.
I love the way you squeal when cold hands touch your back,
and fall asleep on the sofa when we visit your grandparents.
I love it when you say inappropriate things;
I love filling the shocked silence that follows with gentle laughter
and a squeeze of your hand.
I love the way you erode the crotch of your boxers and your jeans
like friction is begging you to become a nudist.
At night,
I sing that I love you.

Life Advice

Lick the custard jug.
Take eight canapes the first time around.
Double, triple and quadruple dip your crackers;
turn out the crisp packet and suck off the salt.
Dip your spoon directly into the jar,
eat the grapes from the cheese board
and chew on the garnish.
Slurp your soup,
take seven sugars in your tea
and drink your coke full-fat.
Gnaw on chicken bones, then
suck your fingers clean.
Always ensure you are first in line
for birthday cake.
Belch appreciatively,
use your sleeve as a napkin,
dig your elbows into the table,
seize the wrong cutlery
in the wrong hands and
refuse to leave without seconds.
Force meteor showers,
cure existence,
evade the certainty of death.
Lick the custard jug.

Trigger Warnings

Bitter Lemons – (Possible Trigger: Abuse)
A Bad Egg – (Possible Trigger: Eating Disorders/ Mental Health)
The Last Supper – Trigger: Suicidal Thoughts
Séance – Trigger: Grief
Pregnancy Scare – (Possible Trigger: Fertility and Abortion)
Aphrodisiac – Trigger: Eating Disorders
What they will never know – Trigger: Eating Disorders

D.D HOLLAND recently graduated from the University of Worcester and is currently studying for her MA at the University of Chichester. Passionate about incorporating Creative Writing into education, she holds workshops in schools and libraries and runs weekly writing classes in local communities. Humour and feminism feature heavily in her work, including her short story collection *The Lady Doth Protest* (Black Pear Press, 2022). Winner of the V. Press Prize for Poetry 2022, *Braised in Wine* is her debut pamphlet.